Animal Adaptations

Diana Noonan

Animal Adaptations

Text: Diana Noonan
Publishers: Tania Mazzeo and Eliza Webb
Series consultant: Amanda Sutera
Hands on Heads Consulting
Editor: Sarah Layton
Project editor: Annabel Smith
Designer: Leigh Ashforth
Project designer: Danielle Maccarone
Permissions researchers: Lumina Datamatics
Production controller: Renee Tome

Acknowledgements
We would like to thank the following for permission to reproduce copyright material:

Front cover: aquamarine4/Adobe Stock Photos; p. 4: (top) Fotos593/Shutterstock.com; (bottom) MH Anderson Photography/Shutterstock.com; p. 5: WildMedia/Shutterstock.com; p. 7: Silken Photography/Shutterstock.com; p. 8: (left) AndreAnita/Shutterstock.com; (right) AB Apana/Moment/Getty Images; p. 9: Ilia Torlin/Shutterstock.com; p. 10: (left) Andrew Haysom/iStock/Getty Images; (right): Bhaveshkumar Panchal/Shutterstock.com; p. 11: Vladimir Wrangel/Shutterstock.com; p. 12: yhelfman/Shutterstock.com; p. 13: (top): Monikasurzin/Adobe Stock Photos; (bottom) Jackie Bale/Moment/Getty Images; p. 14: Danita Delimont/Alamy Stock Photo; p. 15: (top) Tory Kallman/Shutterstock.com; (bottom left) Minden Pictures/Alamy Stock Photo; (bottom right) Kelvin Aitken/Alamy Stock Photo; p. 16: GM Photo Images/Alamy Stock Photo; p. 17: Henk Bogaard/Shutterstock.com; p. 18: Corry Anne/Alamy Stock Photo; p. 19: JAH/iStock/Getty Images; p. 20: (top) mlharing/iStock/Getty Images; (middle) christiannafzger/iStock/Getty Images; (bottom) Mark Conlin/Alamy Stock Photo; title page, p. 21: IHERPHOTO2/Shutterstock.com; p. 22: Wild Art/Shutterstock.com; p. 23: (top) Ian Walker/Alamy Stock Photo; frontcover, (bottom) aquamarine4/Adobe Stock Photos; p. 24: slowmotiongli/Adobe Stock Photos; p. 25 (bottom): Naturfoto-Online/Alamy Stock Photo; p. 26: Robert Kneschke/Shutterstock.com; p. 27: ArieStudio/Shutterstock.com; p. 28: DAVID GRAY/AFP/Getty Images; p. 29 (top) (Index page): Christoph N/Shutterstock.com; p. 29: (bottom) structuresxx/Shutterstock.com; p. 30: pilesasmiles/iStock/Getty Images; back cover: Corry Anne/Alamy Stock Photo.

Every effort has been made to trace and acknowledge copyright. However, if any infringement has occurred, the publishers tender their apologies and invite the copyright holders to contact them.

NovaStar

ISBN 978 0 17 033504 1

Cengage Learning Australia
Level 5, 80 Dorcas Street
Southbank VIC 3006 Australia
Phone: 1300 790 853
Email: aust.nelsonprimary@cengage.com

For learning solutions, visit **cengage.com.au**

Printed in China by 1010 Printing International Ltd
1 2 3 4 5 6 7 29 28 27 26 25

Nelson acknowledges the Traditional Owners and Custodians of the lands of all First Nations Peoples. We pay respect to Elders past and present, and extend that respect to all First Nations Peoples today.

Contents

Our Ever-Changing World

Earth is an ever-changing planet, and its many different environments don't stay the same forever. Changes to an environment can happen quickly or slowly, and they can be harmful or helpful. For example, boiling lava from a volcanic eruption can suddenly set forests or towns on fire, but, over millions of years, rain and wind can turn that same lava into soil that is perfect for growing plants.

The Tungurahua volcano in Ecuador is an active volcano.

Many plants have grown in the volcanic soil near Mount Saint Helens volcano in Washington, USA, since it erupted in 1980.

Many environmental changes are natural, such as when a river is **dammed** by a rockfall and slows to a trickle. Other environmental changes are caused by human activity, such as when a river dries up because farmers have taken too much water from it for **irrigation**.

Whenever environmental changes take place, habitats change, too, and animals are faced with challenges. This is because their bodies and behaviours suit the habitats that they have always lived in.

In a changed habitat, animals may have trouble finding food, shelter and mates. If animals are to survive these challenges, they must be able to **adapt**.

This brown bear's habitat is being destroyed by human activity.

Climate Change and Its Causes

The most rapid and significant environmental changes taking place today are being caused by a rise in Earth's temperature. Human activities that increase **greenhouse gases** in Earth's **atmosphere** are changing the planet's climate. Some of these human activities include forests being destroyed and vehicles **emitting** pollution.

Carbon dioxide, the most common greenhouse gas, works like an invisible blanket around Earth that traps the warmth from the Sun inside our atmosphere. Too much carbon dioxide causes Earth to overheat.

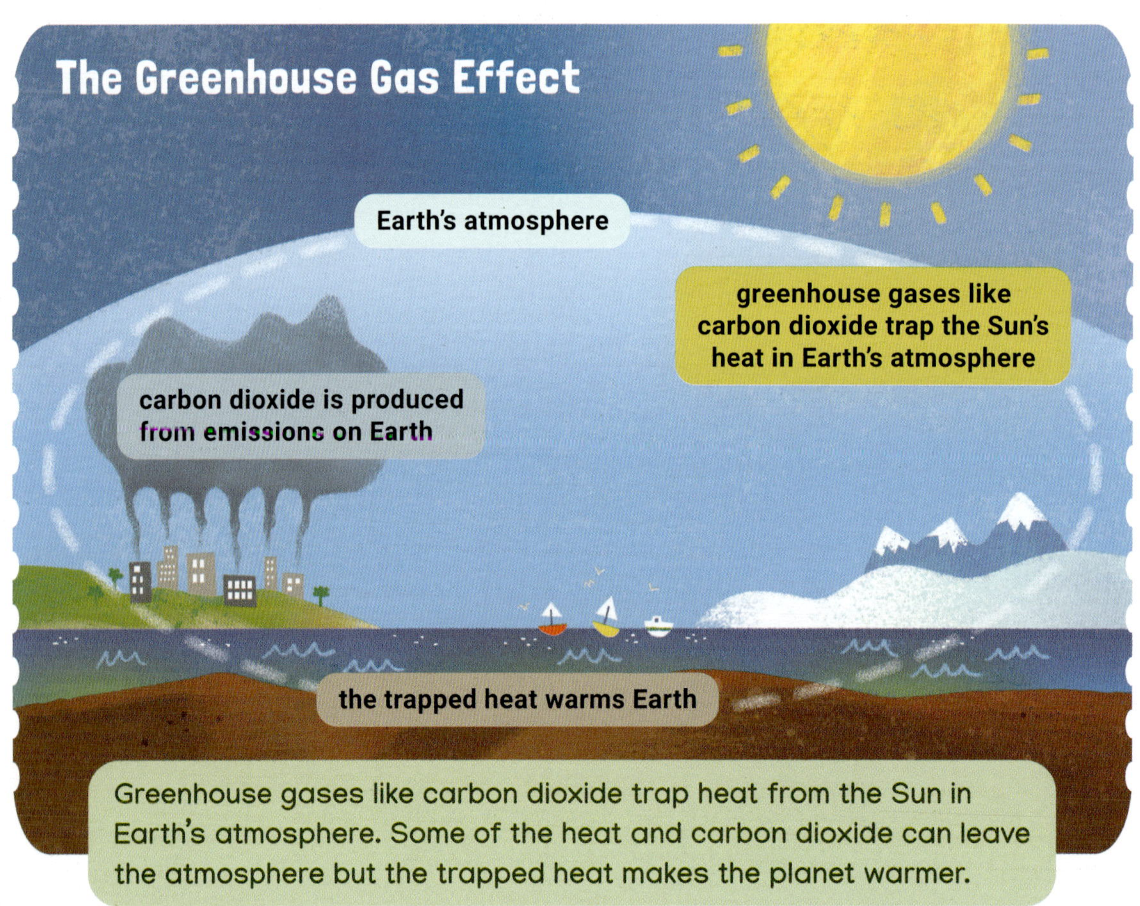

Greenhouse gases like carbon dioxide trap heat from the Sun in Earth's atmosphere. Some of the heat and carbon dioxide can leave the atmosphere but the trapped heat makes the planet warmer.

When Earth overheats, its weather patterns change. Seasons can become much hotter or colder than before. Overheating also causes changes in rainfall, with either much more or much less **precipitation** over longer or shorter periods of time.

Serious weather events are also more common due to climate change – things like damaging and dangerous storms, flooding, droughts, **sea surges**, heatwaves and severe cold snaps. Over time, these weather events **alter** animal habitats.

WEATHER AND CLIMATE – WHAT'S THE DIFFERENCE?

We use the word "weather" to describe how much cold, warmth, moisture and wind an environment experiences over a few minutes or days. The term "climate" describes an environment's weather over many years.

Major flooding events have become more common across Australia.

How Animals Adapt to Climate Change

When climate change alters their habitats, animals can adapt in two main ways. The first is through changing a part of, or feature of, their bodies. For example, if their usual prey has disappeared or become harder to find, the teeth of an animal **species** may become larger or smaller over time. Then, the animal can hunt different kinds of prey. It can take many **generations** before the same change occurs to all animals in a species.

The ears of African elephants are larger than those of Indian elephants to help them stay cool in hotter climates.

African elephant

Indian elephant

The second main way animals adapt is by learning a new behaviour, such as grazing earlier in the day when it's cooler. This kind of **adaptation** can happen within one generation, as animals learn from each other.

EVOLVING BODIES

When the bodies of animal species change over time, we call this process "evolution". These animals can survive in changing environments and have babies, creating further generations.

Kangaroos often graze in the morning or later in the evening to avoid the hotter temperatures during the day.

Today, some animals are not managing to adapt quickly enough to meet the challenges of climate change. When animals can't adapt in time to cope with big changes to their habitats, whole species can face extinction. Those animals that are adapting are doing so in clever ways, but often face other challenges as a result.

ADAPTING OPTION 1

Changing Size

An animal's size, especially the size of its **appendages**, can help it keep a suitable body temperature. As some animals adapt to hotter environments due to climate change, the size of their body parts can slowly change.

Big Beaks

Parrots cool down by losing heat through their beaks. Scientists have shown that the beaks of Australia's red-rumped parrot and gang-gang cockatoo have increased in size since 1871. Scientists think part of the reason for this adaptation is that climate change is warming the birds' habitats. A larger beak provides the birds with a better way of cooling down.

The beaks of the red-rumped parrot and gang-gang cockatoo have increased in size over time, as an adaptation.

red-rumped parrot

gang-gang cockatoo

Big Feet

South African ground squirrels cool down by losing heat through their feet. As climate change has caused the squirrels' grassland and scrub habitat to become hotter, new generations of squirrels have developed larger feet. Scientists think this adaptation is helping the squirrels to keep cool.

South African ground squirrels spend many hours each day looking for food across the vast land. Their big feet have adapted to the hot conditions over time.

ADAPTING OPTION 2

Changing Colour

Animals use their body colours to help them survive. Scientists have noticed that some animals are now changing colour, and they think this may be in response to new challenges caused by climate change.

Attracting a Mate

Some male dragonflies use their black wing patterns to attract a mate, but the dark colour of their wings also absorbs heat. As their habitats grow hotter, some male dragonflies in North America are losing their black wing patterns so that they don't overheat. However, scientists are worried that, in the future, this adaptation may stop female dragonflies from recognising a potential mate. If dragonflies don't mate and breed, their species could become extinct.

The impressive black wing patterns of male North American dragonflies help attract a mate.

Camouflaging

Tawny owls live in forests in many parts of the world. They use their colour to hide from predators and prey. In the past, 70 per cent of tawny owls were grey, and 30 per cent were a reddish-brown colour. Now, half of tawny owls are grey, and half are reddish-brown. Scientists think that the tawny owls' colour-change adaptation is because of the impact climate change is having on their environment. As the owls' habitat warms and receives less snow, reddish-brown is becoming a much better **camouflage** colour for the animals than grey.

Grey tawny owls are able to camouflage in cold, snowy environments, helping to keep them safe from predators.

LOOKING BROWN, FEELING DOWN

Scientists have discovered that grey tawny owls are healthier than reddish-brown ones. If there are too many reddish-brown tawny owls, their species could be at risk.

Scientists think the population of reddish-brown tawny owls has increased due to the warmer climate.

ADAPTING OPTION 3

Changing Diet

Animals' bodies are best suited to eat the food they find in their unique habitats. But as climate change alters the food that is available in their habitats, animals must adapt by eating different foods.

Trying New Foods

In the Arctic winter, Svalbard reindeer eat **lichen**, which grows beneath the snow. They find the lichen by scraping the snow off it with their hooves. But climate change has altered the reindeer's winter habitat by making it warmer. Now, in some places, the snow is melting and then re-freezing as ice, covering the lichen. Unlike the soft snow, this ice is too hard for the reindeer to scrape through to reach their food.

Some reindeer have adapted to this challenge by learning to eat seaweed instead of lichen. However, scientists are concerned that the seaweed doesn't give the reindeer all the **nutrients** they need to stay healthy. If the scientists are correct, this could cause problems for reindeers' survival.

Reindeer in Svalbard, north of Norway, look for food.

Finding New Feeding Grounds

Orca are black-and-white whales with a larger **dorsal fin** than other members of the whale family. Many orca live in cold-water regions, including the Arctic. However, orca can't swim in habitats where there is sea ice floating, as the ice would damage their dorsal fins if they tried to swim through it.

orca

As rising temperatures cause sea ice to melt, orca are now able to swim to areas of the Arctic they previously couldn't reach. When they do, orca hunt different kinds of prey, such as narwhals and bowhead whales. Scientists are concerned that this adaptation could significantly reduce narwhal and bowhead whale numbers. If it does, other animals that hunt narwhals and bowhead whales may not be able to find enough food.

Orca have adapted to preying on the narwhal and the bowhead whale in different parts of the Arctic.

narwhal

bowhead whale

ADAPTING OPTION 4

Making New Hunting Habits

Over many generations, animals have learnt where, when and how to find food. But as climate change alters their habitats, animals must adapt by figuring out new ways to feed themselves.

Changing the Location

Polar bears live in and around the Arctic, where they hunt for seals by waiting beside holes in sea ice. When the seals come up for air through the holes, the polar bears snatch them out of the water. But rising temperatures, caused by climate change, mean there is now less sea ice for the bears to hunt on. In areas where this is happening, some polar bears are starting to hunt for seals on **glaciers**. As global warming increases glacial ice-melting, polar bears will lose even more hunting grounds and may face starvation.

A female polar bear hunts for food in the Arctic.

From Day to Night

Cheetahs are part of the "big cat" family, and they live in mountains and grasslands in several parts of Africa. Cheetahs usually hunt during the day, or at dawn or dusk when it's hot. Other big cat species that live in the same habitat – leopards and lions – hunt at night. However, rising temperatures caused by climate change mean that cheetahs are adapting to hunting at night, too, when it's cooler.

Scientists are concerned that this adaptation may put cheetahs in danger of being preyed upon by leopards and lions. It could also force cheetahs to give up their prey to leopards and lions when they are in danger and go without food themselves. If this happens, it could threaten the cheetahs' survival as a species.

Hunting at night puts cheetahs at risk from other predators.

ADAPTING OPTION 5

Finding New Migration Patterns

Many animals **migrate** seasonally to keep warm, find food and breed in places where their young will thrive. But climate change is now causing seasonal confusion and forcing some animals to change their migration habits.

Escaping the Cold

Monarch butterflies are well-known for their seasonal migrations. In autumn, monarch butterflies in north-eastern America usually migrate to Mexico, where it is warmer. But climate change has altered autumn temperatures in north-eastern America, making it warmer for longer and causing some butterflies to migrate later. By the time these monarch butterflies do leave for Mexico, many of the flowering plants they usually feed on as they fly south have finished blooming. Without this food source along the way, the monarchs' survival may be threatened.

SWEET EATS OR A TOXIC TREAT

Monarch butterflies feed on the sweet nectar found in flowers, especially in native milkweed plants. Milkweed plants are toxic, and by drinking from them, monarch butterflies also become poisonous to eat. The bright orange-and-black wings of the monarch butterfly are a warning to predators that they are toxic.

Monarch butterflies need nectar from plants, like milkweed plants, to survive.

Shortening Migration Periods

Storks are large birds found in many parts of the world. European white storks have historically migrated to parts of Africa in autumn to find warmer temperatures and food. Along the way, many spend time in Spain. But some European white storks are now staying in Spain rather than continuing on to Africa. Scientists think that warmer temperatures, caused by climate change, may be one of the reasons for the storks' shorter migration.

Unfortunately, the white storks in Spain are feeding from waste sites, where they often mistake plastic and rubber rubbish for worms. Storks can die from eating this waste material.

Some European white storks are shortening their migration and stopping in Spain, where they are known to look for food in landfill.

ADAPTING OPTION 6

Changing Breeding Patterns

Animals usually breed with other animals of the same species. Most breed at the same time and in the same place each year. But many of these breeding patterns are changing because of climate change.

Inter-Species Mating

Cutthroat trout are a fish species that lives and breeds in cold-water habitats in the north-east of the USA. But climate change has raised the temperature of the water they usually live in. To escape the warmer water, cutthroat trout are moving to colder streams and lakes where another species of fish – called rainbow trout – live.

Cutthroat and rainbow trout are now breeding with each other, and scientists are worried that the **hybrid** fish (a new species called "cutbow" trout) are producing young that are less likely to survive than their parents. If cutthroat and rainbow trout are replaced by cutbows, and cutbows don't survive, all three species could become extinct.

cutthroat trout

rainbow trout

cutbow trout

New Breeding Grounds

Emperor penguins usually lay their eggs on the same patches of Antarctic sea ice each year. But rising temperatures are changing the birds' habitat, making it less safe for young penguins.

A warmer environment is causing sea ice in the penguins' usual breeding ground to melt and break off into the sea. When it does, the young birds fall into the sea, where they die because their down (soft, baby feathers) is not waterproof. Fortunately, scientists have found that emperor penguins are able to adapt to climate change by moving to new Antarctic breeding grounds.

BREAKING AWAY

In 2022, more than 9000 emperor penguin chicks died in the Antarctic when the sea ice beneath them melted and broke away.

Some Emperor penguins are moving to safer breeding grounds to protect their young.

SUPER AND STRUGGLING ADAPTORS

Scientists around the world have found that some animal species are “super adaptors” and some are “struggling adaptors”.

SUPER ADAPTOR: PIKA

Pikas are small, furry mammals that live in rocky, mountainous areas of North America and Asia. Climate change has altered the habitat of pikas, making it colder in winter and hotter in summer. But scientists believe pikas have quickly adapted to the change by altering their behaviour.

To beat the cold, some pikas have learnt how to curl into a tight ball, so that they lose less heat from their bodies in winter. Some have moved homes to live in forests and on the shores of lakes, where it's warmer in winter.

In summer, some pikas are finding habitats that provide more shade, while others have learnt to eat moss instead of hay. The moss grows all year, so the pikas no longer have to leave the shade to collect hay to store for winter.

Some pikas have found new shady habitats to stay cool in the summer.

ARE WE RELATED?

Pikas belong to the same animal family as hares and rabbits.

Switching their diet from hay to moss has been one way that pikas have adapted to the changing climate.

STRUGGLING ADAPTOR:

WOLVERINES

The wolverine is a strong mammal that looks a bit like a small bear. It is in the same animal family as the weasel and badger.

They live close to the Arctic, where there is snow year-round. Wolverines have many adaptations that allow them to live in this frozen environment.

SOLITARY TRAVELLERS

Wolverines are carnivores that live mostly on their own. They can travel long distances in search of food.

Wolverines can survive in extremely cold weather. Their bodies are designed to quickly use the energy provided from their food. This helps the wolverines keep extra warm in the cold conditions they live in.

However, rising temperatures mean there is now less snow in the wolverines' habitat. Scientists believe wolverines depend on cold conditions so much that they will not be able to adapt quickly enough to survive climate change.

Wolverines need to adapt to warmer climates in order to ensure their survival as a species.

Humans Can Help

Climate change is damaging animal habitats at a faster rate than many animals can adapt, and we humans are to blame. But we can also be part of solving the problem by finding ways to slow climate change and protect endangered species.

Creating and Protecting Reserves

Trees and plants store carbon dioxide in their wood and leaves, which helps to slow climate change. Caring for forest **reserves** and creating new ones protects these carbon dioxide "store houses". Reserves also provide new homes for animals that have had to leave their usual habitats because of climate change or displacement.

Tree-planting days in reserves and parks are a great way to help slow climate change.

Preventing Food Waste

It takes a lot of fuel, such as coal and gas, to produce the food we eat and to transport it to supermarkets. These fuels release harmful gases like carbon dioxide into the atmosphere, which causes climate change. Every year, humans waste about one-third of all the food that is produced in the world. When food is wasted, it ends up in landfill and is buried, creating another harmful gas called **methane** as it decomposes (or breaks down). When we don't waste food, we are helping to slow climate change.

Large piles of food create large amounts of methane as they decompose.

Ways we can prevent food wastage

* Buy fresh food in small quantities, so it's used up before it goes to waste.
* Store food carefully so it lasts longer.
* Put only as much food on a plate as is needed.
* Use food scraps as food for pets.
* Make compost instead of sending food to landfills.

COMPOSTING CORRECTLY

When food is composted correctly, it creates much less methane than it would if it was buried in landfill.

Repairing Environments

Many humans are working hard to care for environments that have been damaged by climate change.

Australia's Great Barrier Reef is home to thousands of different sea animals that live in the reef's coral. But severe storms and rising ocean temperatures, caused by climate change, are damaging the reef. Scientists are exploring ways to re-plant pieces of broken coral on the reef, so that new coral can grow from it.

Scientists explore and inspect coral on the Great Barrier Reef.

Creating Wildlife Corridors

When animals lose their habitats because of extreme weather events, they need to find new homes. As animals move, they need a safe route to travel by and food to eat on the way. Humans can help animals with this by providing safe "wildlife corridors". These corridors are strips of land that resemble an animal's habitat and connect places they need to travel between.

Without wildlife corridors, animals are in danger when travelling near roads and highways.

In Australia, bushfires are becoming more common because of rising temperatures caused by climate change. To help affected animals move safely to new environments, underpasses and overpasses are being built in areas **prone** to bushfires. These wildlife corridors allow animals, such as koalas and wombats, to safely cross busy highways.

More animals are losing their habitats due to the increase of bushfires in Australia.

Managing Environmental Change

Weather events caused by climate change are damaging environments around the world and altering animal habitats. Some animals have developed adaptations in order to survive these changes. However, when animals can't easily adapt, they are at risk and face new challenges.

If animals are to have the best chance of survival, we must try to slow down climate change, so they have enough time to adapt. And we must repair, protect and create habitats to make sure animals have safe places to live.

Glossary

adapt (*verb*)	to adjust to new conditions
adaptation (*noun*)	a changed behaviour or trait that suits a new situation
alter (*verb*)	to change or be impacted
appendages (*noun*)	body parts like legs and arms
atmosphere (*noun*)	the layer of gases around Earth
camouflage (*noun*)	when something blends into its surroundings, making it hard to see
carbon dioxide (*noun*)	a gas in the atmosphere
dammed (*adjective*)	blocked in a way that prevents water from flowing
dorsal fin (*noun*)	a thin body part that extends from the back of a marine animal
emitting (*verb*)	sending something out such as heat or light
generations (*noun*)	periods of time between the birth of animals and the birth of their offspring
glaciers (*noun*)	slow-moving masses of ice
greenhouse gases (*noun*)	the gases that contribute to climate change, especially carbon dioxide and methane
hybrid (*adjective*)	with parents from different species
irrigation (*noun*)	the process of supplying water from rivers or lakes to crops to help them grow
lichen (*noun*)	a very small plant that can grow over rocks
methane (*noun*)	a gas largely produced by some animals and by decomposing landfill waste
migrate (*verb*)	to move from one part of the world to another
nutrients (*noun*)	substances that keep living things alive and healthy
precipitation (*noun*)	rain, hail or snow
prone (*adjective*)	at risk or likely to suffer from something
reserves (*noun*)	pieces of land that are protected areas for animals and plants
sea surges (*noun*)	rising seawater levels caused by storms
species (*noun*)	different types of plants or animals

Index